CAT BREEDS

CAT BREEDS

Judith Steeh

Bison Books

First Published in 1984 by
Bison Books Ltd.
176 Old Brompton Road
London SW5
England

ISBN 0 86124 173 8

Printed in Hong Kong

Reprinted 1985.

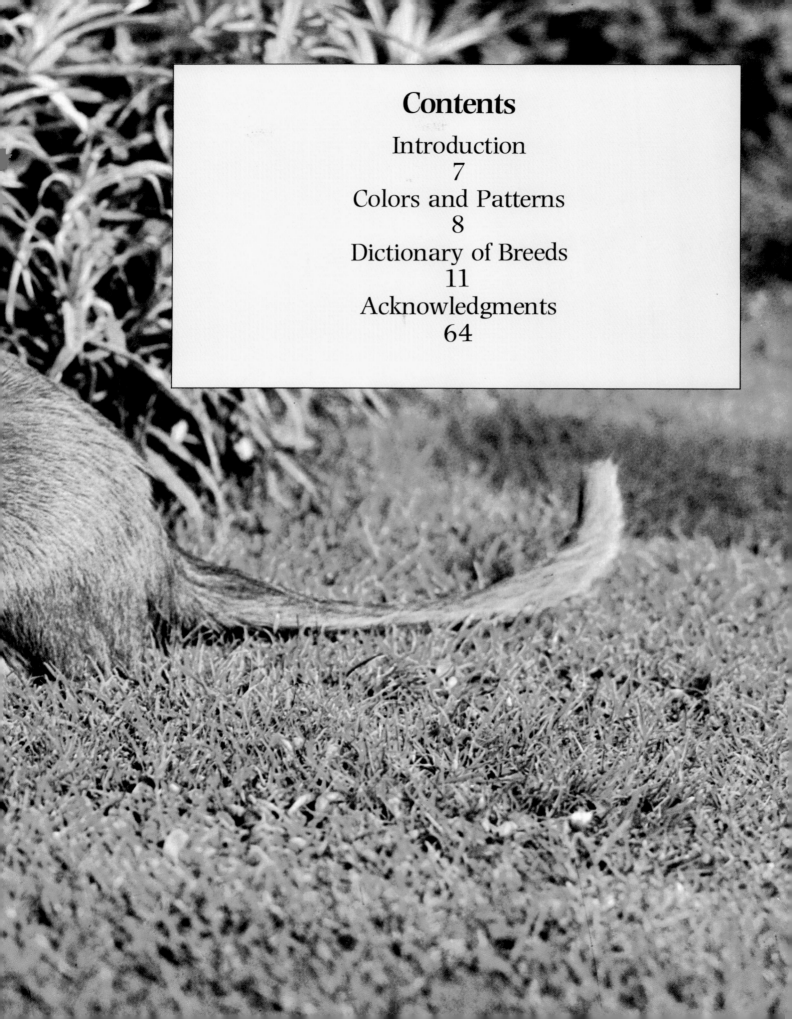

Contents

Introduction

Cats are extraordinary animals, and reactions to them run the gamut from fear and loathing to adoration and worship.

Although few people are true ailurophobes, and even fewer would go to the same lengths as the ancient Egyptians, shaving their eyebrows and mourning for months over the death of a kitten, it is still worth considering how a small, relatively insignificant animal like the domestic cat can inspire such strong reactions.

The most common reason given for disliking cats is their cool, independent, aloof attitude. They seem silent, predatory creatures, accepting sustenance and affection from the misguided humans who keep them, and offering nothing in return. The fact is, of course, that cats *are* mysterious — and it is part of human nature to fear that which we do not understand.

But cat lovers, on the other hand, would point out that it is entirely possible to win a cat's affection and even devotion — and that if companionship with a cat is harder to achieve, that makes it even more valuable. Cats communicate far less with their voices than do dogs, but anyone who takes the trouble to learn their 'body language' will soon discover that they are not nearly so inscrutable.

Colors and Patterns

Most show cats must meet very stringent requirements regarding color and pattern. The descriptions below are adapted from the standards prescribed by the Cat Fanciers' Association, Incorporated (CFA), the largest cat registering organization in the world.

Spectrum A

(a) Solid Colors

Black
The coat must be dense and coal-black from the roots to the tip, with no rusty patches or pale undercoat. Nose leather must be black and paw pads should be black or brown. Eyes should be copper.

Blue
Blue is really a shade of gray. Coat color must be level in tone from nose to tip of tail and from roots to tips of hair. Although the lighter shade (lavender gray) is preferred, a sound darker shade is better than an unsound lighter shade. Nose leather and paw pads should be blue. Eyes should be copper.

Cream
The coat must be an even, buff cream without markings, sound to the roots. Lighter shades are preferable. Nose leather and paw pads should be pink and the eyes copper.

Red
The coat must be a clear, rich red without shading, marking, or tipping and should be even from lips and chin to tail. Nose leather and paw pads should be brick-red and eyes should be copper.

White
The coat should be pure white with no yellowish patches. Nose leather and paw pads should be pink. Eyes can be blue, copper, or one of each. In this last case, the depth of color must be of equal intensity.

(b) Shaded

Chinchilla Silver
The undercoat should be pure white with the fur on the head, back, flanks and tail delicately tipped with black, giving a silvery appearance. The cat's chin, ear tufts, chest and stomach should be pure white although the legs may be slightly shaded. Eyes, lips and nose are outlined in black. Nose leather should be brick-red and paw pads black. Eyes should be green or blue-green.

Shaded Cameo or *Red Shaded*
The undercoat should be white with red tipping, shading down like a mantle from face, sides and tail, from dark on ridge to white on chin, chest, stomach and under the tail. The legs should be the same tone as the face. The general effect is much redder than the Shell Cameo. Nose leather and paw pads must be rose-colored and eyes should be outlined in rose and copper-colored.

Shaded Silver
The undercoat should be white with black tipping shading down like a mantle from face, sides and tail, from dark on the ridge to white on the chin, chest, stomach and under the tail. The general effect is of pewter rather than the silver of the Chinchilla Cameo. Eyes, lips and nose are rimmed in black. Nose leather should be rich red color and paw pads should be black. Eyes must be green or blue-green.

Shell Cameo or *Red Chinchilla*
The undercoat should be white with the fur on the head, back, flanks and tail lightly tipped with red to give a sparkling appearance. Chin, ear tufts, stomach and chest must be white, but face and legs can be very lightly shaded. Nose leather and paw pads should be rose-colored and the copper eyes should be rose-rimmed.

(c) Smoke

Black Smoke
The undercoat should be white with deep black tipping. Motionless, the cat appears solid black, but the white undercoat shows when it moves. Points and mask should be black except for a narrow band of white at the base of each hair which can be seen when the hairs are parted. Ruff and ear tufts should be light silver. Nose leather and paw pads must be black and the eyes, copper.

Blue Smoke
The undercoat must be white with deep blue tipping. Motionless, the cat appears solid blue but the white undercoat shows when it moves. Points and mask are blue except for a narrow band of white at the base of each hair which can be seen when the hairs are parted. The ruff and ear tufts should be white, the nose leather and paw pads should be blue and the eyes, copper.

Red Smoke
The undercoat should be white with deep red tipping. Motionless, the cat appears solid red but the white undercoat shows when it moves. Points and mask are red except for a narrow band of white at the base of each hair which can be seen when the hairs are parted. Eyes are rose-rimmed and golden in color. Nose leather and paw pads are rose.

Previous pages: Shaded Silver Persian.
Top: A close up of an Oriental White Short-hair.
Above: Abyssinian kitten. In the past these cats were known as 'Bunny' or 'Rabbit' cats because of their ticked fur.

Top: Shaded Cameo.
Left: Cream Short-hair.
Below: Smoke Persian
(or Long-hair).

(d) Tabbies
The American CFA recognizes two tabby patterns: classical and mackerel.

Classic Tabby Pattern
The classic tabby pattern is composed of the following elements in a dense, clearly defined color on a contrasting ground.

The legs must be ringed with 'bracelets' coming up to the body and the tail must have even rings on it as well. Several unbroken 'necklaces' must be visible on the neck and chest (the more the better). Frown marks form an intricate 'M' on the forehead. Swirls must be present on the cheeks and an unbroken line should run back from the outer corner of the eye. Vertical lines on the head should run back to the shoulder markings. Shoulder markings in the shape of a butterfly with both upper and lower wings outlined and with dots on the wings must be clearly visible. A vertical line should run down the spine from the butterfly to the tail with parallel vertical lines on either side (called 'spinals'). The three lines should be well-separated by strips of the ground color. A bulls-eye (a large blotch surrounded by two or more unbroken rings) should appear on each side. The two bulls-eyes should be identical. A double, vertical line of spots, or 'buttons' should run along the chest and stomach.

Mackerel Tabby Pattern
In many respects the markings are similar to the classic tabby pattern. Although the lines are much narrower, they must still be dense and clearly defined. As in the classic pattern there are 'bracelets' on the legs, rings on the tail, 'necklaces' on the neck and chest and an 'M' on the forehead with unbroken lines running back from the eyes and from the head to the shoulders. However, in the mackerel tabby pattern, the spine lines run together, forming a narrow saddle while narrow pencilings run around the body. The pattern on the body should look like clouds in the sky.

All tabby colors outlined below appear in both classic and mackerel patterns.

Blue Tabby
The pale ivory ground color of the coat has deep blue markings with fawn overtones or 'patina' appearing over the entire coat. Nose leather is dusty rose and paw pads are rose-colored. Eyes are copper.

Brown Tabby
The copper-brown ground color has dense black markings and the lips and chin should be the same color as the rings around the eyes. The back of the leg is black from paw to heel. Nose leather is brick-red and paw pads should be black or brown. Eyes should be copper.

Cameo Tabby
The ground color should be off-white with red markings. Nose leather and paw pads should be rose-red and eyes, copper.

Cream Tabby
The ground color should be very pale cream with buff or cream markings that are dark enough for good contrast. Nose leather and paw pads should be pink and the eyes, copper.

Red Tabby
The ground color should be red with deep red markings. The cat should have brick-red nose leather, pink paw pads and copper eyes.

Silver Tabby
The ground color should be pale, clear silver with dense black markings. The cat should have brick-red nose leather, black paw pads and green or hazel eyes.

(e) Parti-colors
Bi-color
The coat of a Bi-colored cat should be black, blue, cream or red with white feet, legs, underparts, chest and muzzle. White under the tail and around the neck is acceptable and a blaze on the face in the form of an inverted 'V' is desirable. Eyes should be copper.

Blue-Cream
In this case the coat should be blue with clearly defined, well-broken patches of cream on the body, legs, tail and head. Paler shades are preferred. Eyes should be copper.

Calico
Here the coat should be white with well-defined, unbrindled patches of red and black. White predominates on the underparts. Eyes should be copper. (Small red and black spots on white are characteristics of the unrecognized Harlequin.)

Dilute Calico
The coat should be white with well-defined, unbrindled patches of blue and cream; white predominates on the underparts. Eyes should be copper.

Tortoiseshell
The coat must be black with well-defined, unbroken, distinct patches of red and cream on body, head, legs and tail. A red or cream blaze from forehead to nose is desirable. Eyes are copper.

Spectrum B

Spectrum B describes the colorpoint pattern and the four classic point colors. For other colors, see Colorpoint Shorthair.

The colorpoint pattern consists of a basic body color and a contrasting point color. The points appear on the cooler extremities of the cat, and have sometimes been called 'temperature points.'

The points, which must be well-defined, of a contrasting color, and of the same color density, are the mask, ears, feet, tail, and sex organs. There should not be any ticking or white hairs in the points.

The mask should cover the entire face, including the whisker pads, and be connected to the ears by 'tracings'; it should not, however, extend over the top of the head. Eyes are vivid blue for all colors.

Blue Point
Body is a glacial, bluish white, shading to white on the underparts. Points are blue; nose leather and paw pads are slate-blue.

Chocolate Point
Body is ivory, with no shading. Points are warm, even milk-chocolate; nose leather and paw pads are cinnamon.

Lilac Point (Frost Point)
Body is glacial white with no shading. Points are frosty gray with a pink tinge; nose leather is pale lilac and paw pads are cold pink.

Seal Point
Body is cream with warm, pale fawn shading to the back. Points are dense, dark, seal-brown; nose leather and paw pads are the same color as the points. Faults include grayness in the coat, a dark smudge on the belly or throat, white toes, or brindling in the points.

Right: Blue Burmese. Below: Birman kitten. Center below: This Siamese kitten is similar in type to the Burmese but with a less solid body and a more pointed face. Bottom: Long-haired Colorpoint or Himalayan.

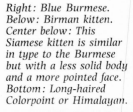

Dictionary of Breeds

Abyssinian

Abyssinians — affectionate, highly intelligent cats with small, melodious voices — make delightful pets. They dislike close confinement and always take a keen interest in their surroundings.

With its medium-sized, well-muscled, short-haired body, the Abyssinian is perhaps the most feral-looking of all the domestic breeds. The shape of its body is Oriental, like that of the Siamese, but not as long. It is lithe and graceful, with a fairly long tapering tail, slender legs and neat oval feet.

The head is a rounded, medium, well-proportioned wedge with longish ears that are broad at the base and sharp at the tip. Eyes are large, almond-shaped, and very expressive.

Abyssinians have very soft, dense, resiliant coats. Two colors — Ruddy (the most common) and Red — are recognized by cat fanciers; a Cream Abyssinian has also been bred. A long-haired Abyssinian, the *Somali*, has been recognized as a breed.

Ruddy Abyssinian

The coat of the Ruddy Abyssinian is reddish brown with each hair ticked with two or three shades of black or dark brown. The undercoat next to the skin is ruddy, with the outer tips of the hairs being the darkest shade. Fur on the stomach and the inside of the forelegs is a lighter shade that harmonizes with the overall body color; the back of the hind legs is black and the chin is often white. Eyes are gold or green (sometimes hazel), the nose is red, and paw pads are black or brown.

Red Abyssinian

This breed's coat is a rich, warm, coppery-red, ticked with chocolate brown. Deeper shades of red are preferable.

Right: Ruddy Abyssinian.
Inset: American Short-hair.

American Short-hair

Once called simply the domestic short-hair, this all-American cat traveled to the New World on the *Mayflower*, and has been an integral part of American life ever since. It is a working cat — a solid citizen, a good companion, and infinitely adaptable — that now has a full pedigree from the Cat Fanciers' Association (CFA).

The American Short-hair is a well-built cat with the rippling muscles and latent power of the trained athlete. It has a powerful medium-to-large body with heavy shoulders and a well-developed chest, firm strong legs of medium length, and a medium-length tail that tapers from a thick base and ends bluntly.

The head is large and well-proportioned, slightly longer than it is wide. The muzzle is square, the chin firm, the cheeks full and the nose medium (snub noses are considered faults). The medium size, wide-set ears are slightly rounded. Eyes are large and round, set well apart, and slant slightly at the outer edge. They should be bright, clear, and alert.

The American Short-hair conformation covers a wide range of breeds, including the Chinchilla and Shaded Silver. It is recognized in all colors and patterns of Spectrum A (see Colors and Patterns).

Angora

The Angora is small to medium in size with a small head and tapering, upright ears. The eyes are large, almond-shaped, slightly slanted, and wide-set; they can be either blue, amber, or one of each color (some blue-eyed Angoras suffer from deafness). The tail is long, full, and tapering, and should not be kinked. When the cat is relaxed and moving it carries its tail horizontally over its body, almost touching the ears. Paw pads, nose leather, and lips are pink.

The coat should be fine, medium length, and soft with a silky finish. There are tufts of hair between the toes. Only white Angoras are presently eligible for the CFA Championship competition, though they have been bred in other colors from Spectrum A (see Colors and Patterns).

Balinese

The Balinese is basically a long-haired Siamese. The mutation appeared in America in litters of purebred Siamese and it was found that when the mutations were mated they bred true. They were recognized as a breed in the United States in 1963.

Balinese have voices and characters similar to Siamese cats, but are considered by some to be less demanding. Like the Siamese, too, they are highly intelligent and very affectionate animals.

Balinese cats should not be confused with Persians or Himalayans, which have much longer coats. The coat on a Balinese is soft, silky, and about two inches long, requiring much less attention than that of other long-haired cats.

The Balinese body is tight, slim and elegant,

Balinese cat and her kitten.

with fine bones and firm muscles. Balinese cats should be medium in size and the same width at the shoulders and hips. Legs are long and slim, with the hind legs longer than the front. The long, thin tail tapers to a point; the tail hair spreads out like a plume.

The head is a long, tapering wedge that starts from the nose and flares out to the ears in straight lines. Ears are very large and pointed, and continue the lines of the wedge. Eyes are medium-sized and almond-shaped, of a deep, vivid blue. They should never be crossed. Balinese have fairly long necks.

The Balinese falls under Spectrum B (see Colors and Patterns). Points and mask should be clearly defined without brindling or white hairs. The whole face should be covered by the mask. The coat will probably darken as the cat gets older, but the shading should remain even.

Bi-colored Persian

The Bi-colored Persian (often called Parti-colored Persian) was originally shown only in black and white and entered under the name Magpie. It was recognized as a separate breed in the mid-1960s. Bi-colored Persians are important in breeding long-haired Calico Cats.

Conformation should be that of the Persian: big, cobby body with short thick legs, broad head and short bushy tail.

The coat should be long, flowing, and silky. It must combine white with one other solid color; tabby markings are considered faults.

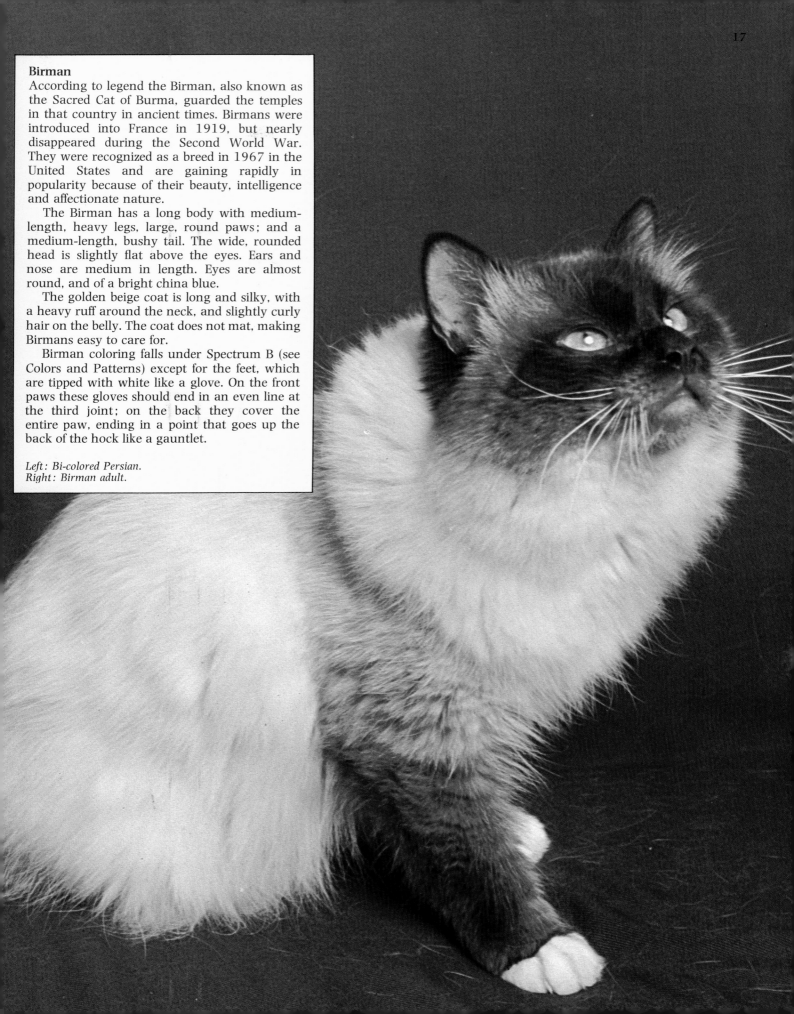

Birman

According to legend the Birman, also known as the Sacred Cat of Burma, guarded the temples in that country in ancient times. Birmans were introduced into France in 1919, but nearly disappeared during the Second World War. They were recognized as a breed in 1967 in the United States and are gaining rapidly in popularity because of their beauty, intelligence and affectionate nature.

The Birman has a long body with medium-length, heavy legs, large, round paws; and a medium-length, bushy tail. The wide, rounded head is slightly flat above the eyes. Ears and nose are medium in length. Eyes are almost round, and of a bright china blue.

The golden beige coat is long and silky, with a heavy ruff around the neck, and slightly curly hair on the belly. The coat does not mat, making Birmans easy to care for.

Birman coloring falls under Spectrum B (see Colors and Patterns) except for the feet, which are tipped with white like a glove. On the front paws these gloves should end in an even line at the third joint; on the back they cover the entire paw, ending in a point that goes up the back of the hock like a gauntlet.

Left: Bi-colored Persian.
Right: Birman adult.

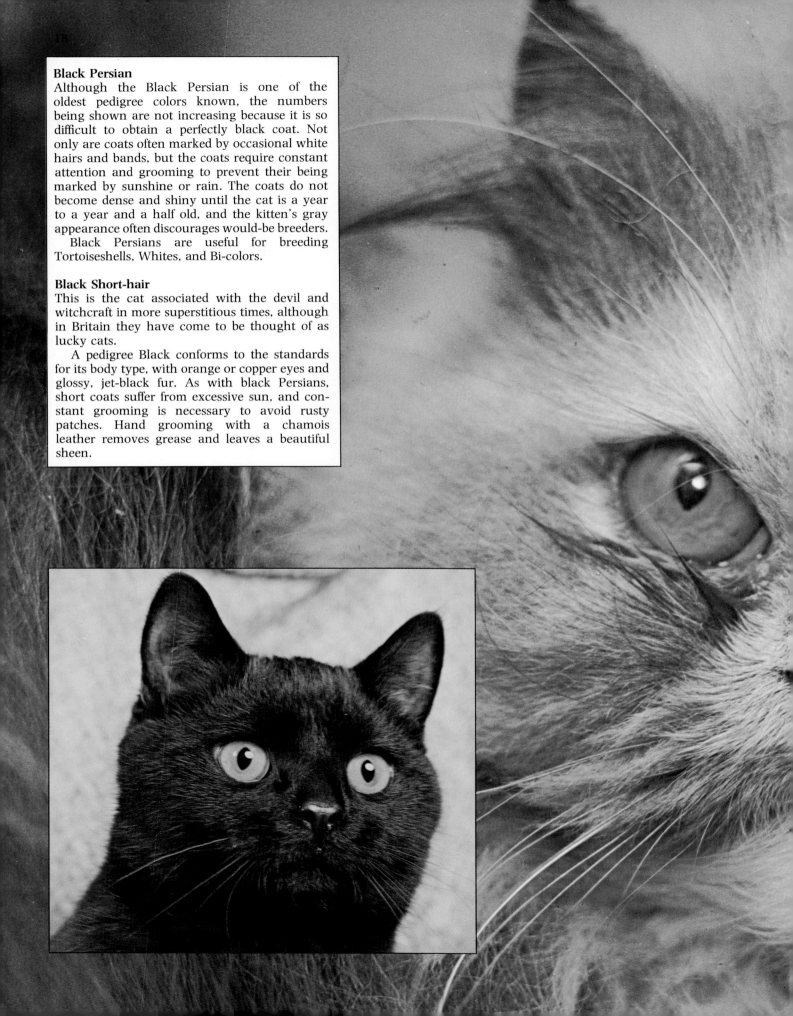

Black Persian

Although the Black Persian is one of the oldest pedigree colors known, the numbers being shown are not increasing because it is so difficult to obtain a perfectly black coat. Not only are coats often marked by occasional white hairs and bands, but the coats require constant attention and grooming to prevent their being marked by sunshine or rain. The coats do not become dense and shiny until the cat is a year to a year and a half old, and the kitten's gray appearance often discourages would-be breeders.

Black Persians are useful for breeding Tortoiseshells, Whites, and Bi-colors.

Black Short-hair

This is the cat associated with the devil and witchcraft in more superstitious times, although in Britain they have come to be thought of as lucky cats.

A pedigree Black conforms to the standards for its body type, with orange or copper eyes and glossy, jet-black fur. As with black Persians, short coats suffer from excessive sun, and constant grooming is necessary to avoid rusty patches. Hand grooming with a chamois leather removes grease and leaves a beautiful sheen.

Above: Blue Cream Persian.
Inset: Black Short-hair.

Blue Cream Persian

Blue Cream Persians are very attractive cats, produced by mating Blues and Creams. Males are rare and are always sterile. Body should conform to that of the Persian; eyes should be large, round, and of a copper or dark orange color. (See also Colors and Patterns).

Blue Cream Short-hair

As with the Blue Cream Persian, this variety is almost entirely female; males are always sterile. Again the type is the result of Blue and Cream matings, though it sometimes appears in Tortoiseshell litters if both parents carry blue genes.

Blue Cream Short-hairs should conform to the standards for their body type, except that eyes may only be copper, orange, or yellow.

They are very popular cats, both for their pleasant personalities and the large variety of kittens they can produce.

Blue Persian

The Blue Persian has been important in the improved breeding of nearly all solid-color Persians and in the development of new colors such as Colorpoints. It is one of the most attractive and photogenic breeds.

Lighter shades are preferred, but evenness of color is more important than tone. White hairs in the coat, green eye rims, and kinked tails are considered faults. Kittens are often born with tabby markings, but lose these quickly as they grow up. Although this cat should have a snub nose, one that is too short indicates overbreeding. The head should be broad, the ears small, the eyes round and copper-colored, and the ruff large and well-developed.

Blue Short-hair

There are several recognized breeds of Blue Short-hairs. Each breed has certain characteristics which set it apart from the others (for example, each has differently colored eyes). If a cat is of poor quality, however, these distinctions become blurred and even experts cannot always be sure of the actual breed.

Recognized breeds of Blue Short-hairs are:

Blue American Short-hair
Blue Burmese
Blue Exotic Short-hair
Blue Japanese Bobtail
Blue Manx 'Longie'

Blue Oriental Short-hair
British Blue
Chartreux
Korat
Maltese
Russian Blue

Bombay

This shiny black hybrid is a recent addition to the show scene. It was originally produced by mating American Short-hairs and Burmese.

The standards for body type are almost exactly the same as those for the Burmese: a medium-size, muscular body with legs in proportion and a straight, medium-length tail; a round head with a short, well-developed muzzle; wide-set ears that are broad at the base and slightly rounded at the tips; and round, wide-set eyes.

In judging, 55 percent of the Bombay Standard is concerned with coat and color — more than any other breed. The coat must be fine, short, and satiny, and lie very close to produce a 'patent leather' sheen. Fur must be black to the roots. Nose leather and paw pads are black. Eyes are yellow to deep copper.

Left: Blue Persian.
Below: Sable Burmese.

Burmese

Burmese are hardy, sociable cats that make excellent companions.

The Burmese is a medium-size cat with heavier bones and more muscle than its size would indicate; a round, strong chest; and a straight back. Legs are slender, with the hind legs longer than front legs. Paws are round. The tail is medium, slender, and straight.

The head is round, with a blunt wedge-shaped muzzle and a full face. There is a strong lower jaw and a distinct nose break. Ears are medium in size, broad at the base and slightly rounded at the tip; they are wide-set and tip slightly forward. The wide-set eyes are a rounded almond shape.

Sable (or 'Brown') Burmese is the only color recognized by the CFA in America. Because of its hybrid ancestry, however, other colors have emerged; blue, champagne, and platinum are the most common, and have been recognized by other organizations.

Blue Burmese

This color was achieved by mating the lighter-colored kittens from a Sable Burmese litter, and the required conformation is the same as for the Sable Burmese. The coat should be a bluish-gray with a silvery tinge on face, ears, and feet; the back and tail are slightly darker. Eyes are yellow; they can have a slight greenish tinge, but should never be a distinct green. Paw pads are gray and nose leather is dark gray. Kittens have tabby markings which fade.

Blue Cream Burmese

This is a female-only type, with the standard Burmese conformation. Nose leather and paw pads are blotched blue and pink.

Champagne Burmese

The coat of this popular type should be a warm, even, milk-chocolate color; ears and mask can be slightly darker. Paw pads are slightly redder and nose leather slightly browner than the coat.

Cream Burmese

The Cream Burmese is a rich cream color, paler on the underparts, darker on back and tail, and darker still on the ears. Slight tabby markings on the face are accepted. Nose leather and paw pads are pink.

Platinum Burmese

The coat should be dove gray with a frosted, pinkish sheen, slightly darker on ears and mask. Nose leather and paw pads are a lavender pink. This variety results from mating two Champagne Burmese that carry a blue gene, or a Champagne and a Blue.

Platinum Tortie Burmese

The colors, platinum and cream, should be distributed without barring. Conformation is more important than coloration or markings.

Red Burmese

The coat color should be a golden red, fading to tangerine on the underparts. Eyes are darker and slight tabby markings are acceptable. Nose leather and paw pads are chocolate but pink is acceptable.

Sable Burmese

The Sable Burmese has a close-lying, satin-textured coat of a deep, rich, sable brown that gradually becomes slightly lighter on the underparts. Otherwise the color is absolutely even, with no shadings or markings. Kittens are sometimes coffee-colored, with shadow markings and a few white hairs. Nose leather and paw pads are brown. Eyes should range from yellow to gold; green eyes are considered faults and blue eyes disqualify the cat on the show bench — as do kinked tails or white spots in the coat.

Tortoiseshell Burmese

This is a female-only type. Burmese conformation is more important than coat color, which is a mingled or blotched mixture of brown, cream, and red. Legs and tail are often a solid color. Nose leather and paw pads are plain or blotched, chocolate or pink.

Left: Brown Burmese.
Above: The ever-popular Blue Burmese.

24

Calico Cat

Calico cats come in both long- and short-haired varieties. The Calico Short-hair is believed to have originated in Spain, and is one of the earliest known varieties.

The Calico is a difficult cat to reproduce since it is an almost all-female type. A Black or White male makes the best stud, but breeding is a chancy matter at best. Care should be taken to avoid mating cats with white hairs or tabby markings.

Conformation and coat quality should be that of the appropriate Persian or Short-hair standard.

Coloration requirements vary, but the CFA and most other associations call for predominantly white underparts and black and red patches. The patches must always be clearly defined and free from brindling. Feet and legs, the whole underside of the body, tail, chest, and most of the neck should be white with splashes on the nose. The white should also come up to cover the lower parts of the sides. Eyes are orange- or copper-colored; hazel eyes are sometimes permitted in short-hairs.

Dilute Calico

Dilute Calicos were the result of mating Calicos and Blue and White Bi-coloreds.

Left: Calico Cat.
Above: Smoke Cameo.

Cameo

Cameos are attractive long-haired cats developed in America during the 1950s and recognized in 1960.

Coloration is more important than conformation which should be the same as for other Persians.

Cameos are found with shaded colors – Shell Cameo and Shaded Cameo – in Smokes, and with tabby markings. There is also a Tortoiseshell Cameo that is slowly gaining recognition; it has a silvery white undercoat and standard tortoiseshell markings, with ticking of red and cream or black and blue.

Tabby Cameo coats are also recognized in Exotic Short-hairs by some governing bodies.

Chartreux
The sturdy Chartreux is the indigenous Blue Short-hair of France, and is thought to have been brought to that country from South Africa by Carthusian monks.

It is a gentle, affectionate, and intelligent cat — and is also a skilled hunter of rodents.

Left: Chartreux.
Below: Chinchilla kitten.
Overleaf: Chinchilla.

Chinchilla

This small, long-haired cat was created almost a century ago in Britain from a cross between a Silver Tabby and a Smoke; in America it is often called Silver Persian. Many consider it to be the most beautiful of the long-haired cats.

Conformation should basically be that of other long-haired varieties, except for its lighter bone structure which gives it a dainty appearance.

The head is round and broad; the snub nose has a brick-red tip; and the ears are wide-set and well-tufted. The eyes should be large, emerald or blue-green in color. The tail should be short and bushy.

The coat should be thick, long, and silky, pure white on the underparts, chin and ear tufts. All the other hairs are delicately tipped with black, giving the animal a shimmering, silvery appearance. Heavy tipping, yellow patches, or brown, cream, or tabby markings are considered faults. Kittens are born with darker fur and tabby markings which eventually disappear. (See also Colors and Patterns).

Blue Chinchilla

This cat, the result of mating a Chinchilla with a Blue Persian, is being developed in England, but has not yet been recognized as a separate variety. The adult cat has a pure white undercoat, tipped on the back, tail, flanks, head, and ears with blue-gray. Legs may have ticking. Eyes can be orange or amber.

Colorpoint Short-hair

The Colorpoint Short-hair is the result of the desire of breeders in America to extend the basic colorpoint pattern beyond the four classic colors (Seal Point, Chocolate Point, Blue Point, and Lilac Point). This was accomplished by mating Siamese and American Short-hairs, to produce a cat that retained the Siamese conformation and colorpoint factor, but acquired additional colors and patterns from the American Short-hair.

The success of this idea is an outstanding example of the art of breeding. In addition, the Colorpoint Short-hair is a warm, friendly cat that makes an excellent pet.

The Colorpoint Short-hair should be identical to the Siamese in every respect save color. The cats are divided into three categories: Solid Color Point, Lynx (or Tabby) Point, and Parti-Color Point. Eyes in all cases should be deep blue.

Solid Color Point

(a) *Red Point:* Experimental breeding between Seal Point Siamese females and Red Tabby Short-hair males began during the Second World War; Red Points were recognized in America in 1956. The body should be clear white with any shading the same color as the points which are deep reddish brown. Nose leather and paw pads are flesh or coral.

(b) *Cream Point:* As above, except that the points are apricot.

Lynx Point

Also known as Silver Point Siamese, Shadow Point, and Tabby Colorpoint Short-hair. Lynx Points tend to have gentler natures than other Siamese.

In all of the colors described below, the body color may be lightly shaded. The points contain distinct, darker shaded bars separated by a lighter background color. The ears are the basic point color with a paler, thumbprint-shaped mark in the center.

(a) *Blue Lynx Point:* Cold, bluish white to platinum-gray body, shading to a lighter color on stomach and chest, with deep blue-gray points on the lighter ground. Nose leather is slate or pink, edged in slate; paw pads are slate-colored.

(b) *Chocolate Lynx Point:* Ivory body with warm mild chocolate points on lighter ground. Nose leather is cinnamon or pink, edged in cinnamon; paw pads are cinnamon.

(c) *Lilac Lynx Point:* Glacial white body and frosty gray points with a pinkish tone on a lighter ground. Nose leather is lavender pink or pink, edged in lavender pink; paw pads are lavender pink.

(d) *Red Lynx Point:* White body with deep red points on a lighter ground. Nose leather and paw pads are flesh-color or coral.

(e) *Seal Lynx Point:* Cream or pale fawn body color, with seal brown points on a lighter ground. Nose leather is seal brown or pink, edged in seal brown; paw pads are seal brown.

Parti-color Point

In all colors the points are a basic solid color mottled with patches of one or more contrasting colors. A blaze on the mask is desirable; when such a blaze is present the nose leather may be mottled.

(a) *Blue Cream Point:* Cold bluish white to platinum-gray body, lighter on chest and stomach; deep blue-gray points uniformly mottled with cream. Nose is slate-colored although flesh or coral mottling is permitted with a blaze. Paw pads are slate but flesh or coral mottling is permitted where the point color extends into the pads.

(b) *Chocolate Cream Point:* Ivory body; warm milk chocolate points uniformly mottled with cream. Nose leather is cinnamon but flesh or coral mottling is permitted with a blaze. Paw pads are cinnamon but flesh or coral mottling is permitted where the point color mottling extends into the pads.

(c) *Lilac Cream Point:* Glacial white body; frosty gray points with a pinkish tone uniformly mottled with pale cream. Nose leather is lavender pink although flesh or coral mottling is permitted with a blaze. Paw pads are lavender pink but flesh or coral mottling is permitted where the point color extends into the pads.

(d) *Seal Tortie Point:* Pale fawn to cream body, shading to a lighter color on chest and stomach; seal points uniformly mottled with red and cream. Nose leather is seal brown, and flesh or coral mottling is permitted with a blaze. Paw pads are seal brown, and flesh or coral mottling is permitted where the point color mottling extends into the pads.

Right: Lynx Point — an excellent example of one type of Colorpoint Short-hair.

*Below: The Cornish
Si-Rex is the result of the
mating of a Cornish Rex
and a Siamese.
Right: Cream Persian or
Long-hair.*

Cornish Rex
The body of the Cornish Rex is Oriental — medium in length, slender, and strong — resembling that of the Siamese. Legs are long and straight with oval paws and the tail is long and tapering.

The head is medium in size, wedge-shaped, and narrowing to a strong chin. In profile the head is flat, with a sharp angle at the forehead and a straight line from forehead to nose. The large ears are set high and are wide at the base with rounded tips; eyes are medium and oval.

The coat is short and curly, and can be any color in Spectrum A and some variations from Spectrum B (see Colors and Patterns). It is especially thick on the back and tail, giving the animal a plushy appearance. The curliness is due to the absence of guard hairs. Any white markings must be symmetrical except in the Calico.

Cream Persian
This popular variety originated from mating Blues and Reds.

The body should be solid and conform to Persian standards. The tail should be short, but flowing.

The coat is long and dense, without white hairs, and should not be too red or too harsh in texture. When the cat is molting the coat tends to darken, and regular brushing is required to maintain its cream color.

In mating, the occasional introduction of a Blue may help keep the pale cream color and avoid the 'hot' red tinge mentioned above. When a Cream is mated with a Blue male, the litter can contain Cream males and Blue Cream females. A Cream male mated with a Blue female may produce Blue male kittens and Blue Cream females. Female Creams are usually obtained by mating a Cream male with a Cream or Blue Cream female.

Cream Short-hair

Cream Short-hairs are beautiful and much-admired cats, but are very difficult to breed to standard.

Body conformation should be that of the Short-hair. Kittens are often born with barred markings which they may or may not lose as they mature; bars, stripes, and especially ringed tails are the most common faults in adult show animals.

Below: Cream Short-hair kitten.

Cymric

The Cymric is a recognized breed and has been developed in America since 1960.

It is a hybrid, probably produced by mating a short-haired Manx with a Persian (though some consider it to be a mutation).

Except for its long coat, the Cymric should conform to the Manx standard. Its most notable feature is its rounded rump, created by its short back, high hindquarters, and taillessness. The head is long and round with prominent cheeks; the nose is long; the ears are wide tapering to a point at the tip.

All colors and patterns of Spectrum A are possible.

Below: Devon Rex.
Right: Bronze Egyptian
Mau.

Devon Rex
Good-tempered and quiet, the Devon Rex makes an excellent pet for apartment dwellers.

The Devon Rex is of medium length with long slim legs, a wide chest and slender neck, and a long, thin, tapering tail.

The head is wedge-shaped with a flat skull, full cheeks, and a strong chin. There is a definite nose break. Whiskers and eyebrows are crinkled, and of medium length. Ears are large. The large eyes are oval and wide-set and should match the coat in color.

The coat is thinner than that of the Cornish Rex. It should be short, without guard hairs, fine, wavy, and soft. The Devon Rex is bred in most colors and patterns of Spectrum A and some of B.

Egyptian Mau
The Egyptian Mau — the only domesticated spotted cat — was developed during the 1950s from cats imported from Cairo, Egypt. It is still relatively rare, and has been only provisionally accepted for CFA shows.

The Mau's body should strike a nice balance between the compact Burmese and the lithe, elegant Siamese. It is graceful and medium in size with well-developed muscles. The hind legs are longer than the front legs; paws are small and almost round. The tail is medium in length, thick at the base and tapering slightly. Bodies that are too cobby or Oriental and tails that are short or 'whip' are considered faults.

The head is a modified, slightly rounded wedge without any flat planes. There is a slight rise from the bridge of the nose to the forehead which in turn flows into the arched neck without a break. The muzzle is rounded, and allowances are made for broad heads or stud jowls in males.

Ears are large, broad at the base, moderately pointed and alert. Hair on the ears should be short and close-lying, and the ears can be tufted. The inner ear is a delicate, translucent shell-pink.

The eyes should be large, almond-shaped, and slightly slanted. All colors of Egyptian Mau have light, gooseberry-green eyes; a slight amber cast is permissible.

The coat of an Egyptian Mau should be medium but long enough for two bands of ticking separated by lighter bands of color to be visible. It is fine, silky, and resiliant.

There are some similarities between the Egyptian Mau and the Tabby pattern. The forehead carries the distinctive 'M' (or 'scarab') and frown marks which form lines between the ears. These lines run down the back of the neck, breaking into elongated 'spots' along the spine and coming together again at the rear haunches to become a dorsal stripe that continues to the tip of the tail.

There are two 'mascara' lines on the cheeks. One starts at the corner of each eye and runs along the contour of the cheek; the other starts at the center of the cheek and curves up to almost meet the first.

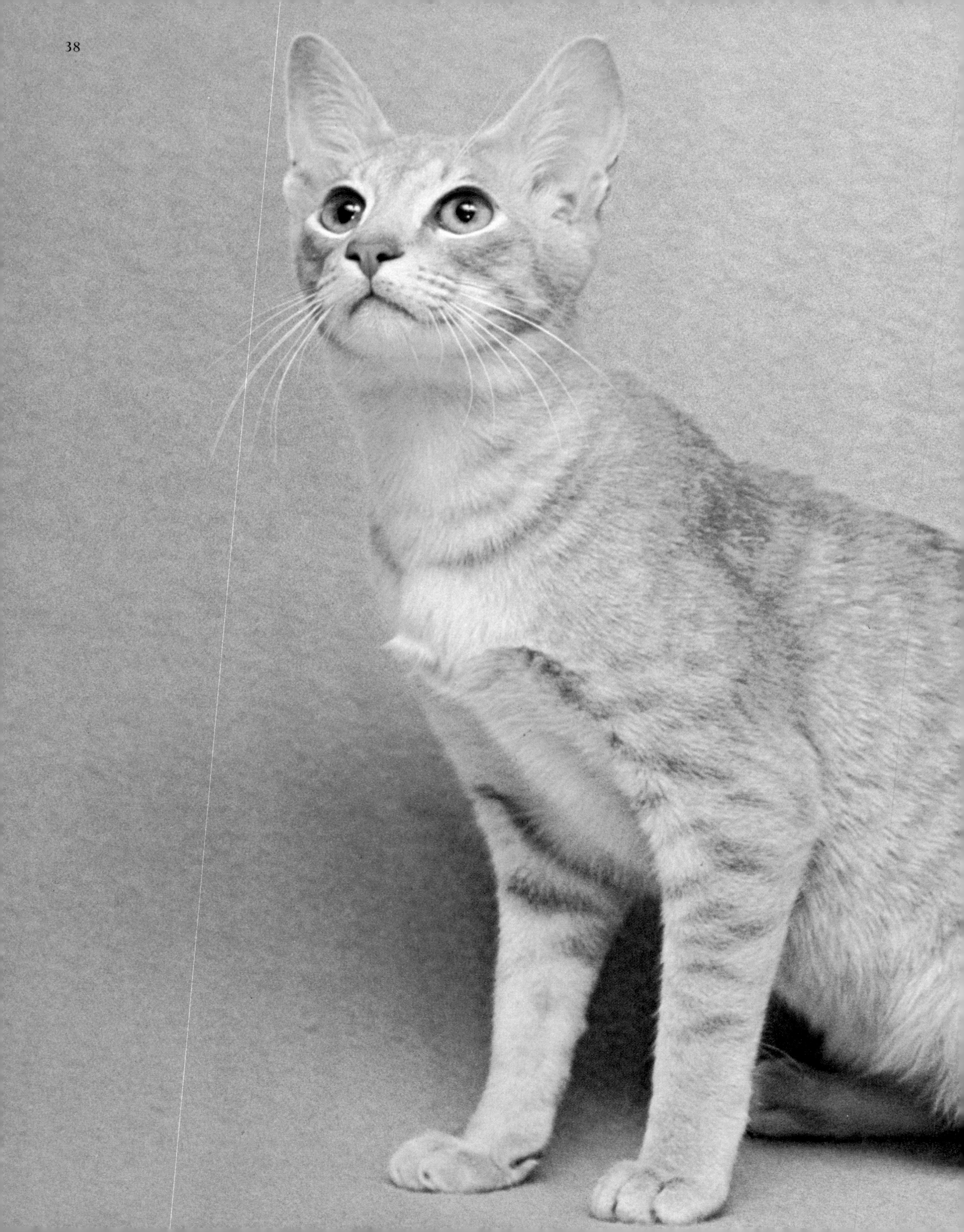

The tail is heavily ringed (banded); there are one or more necklaces (preferably broken at the center) on the upper chest; and the upper forelegs are heavily barred. On the body random spots of varying size and shape should be evenly distributed, though the pattern need not be the same on both sides. The spots should be distinct, and may not run together to form a mackerel tabby pattern. There are 'vest pocket' spots on the underside of the body.

Transitional spots and stripes on the haunches and upper hind legs break into bars on the thighs and spots on the lower hind legs.

The Egyptian Mau is recognized in three colors: Bronze, Silver, and Smoke.

Bronze Mau
The ground color of the Bronze Mau's coat is light bronze becoming darkest over the shoulders and shading to tawny buff on the sides and creamy ivory on the underparts; markings are dark brown. Backs of the ears are tawny pink and tips are dark brown. Nose, lips, and eyes are outlined in dark brown; bridge of nose is ocher. The upper throat, chin, and the area around the nostrils should be creamy white. Nose leather is brick-red; paw pads are black or dark brown. There is black or dark brown hair between the toes and the same color extends slightly beyond the paws on the hind feet.

Silver Mau
The coat of the Silver Mau has a pale silver ground color with charcoal markings. Backs of the ears are grayish pink, and tips are black. The upper throat, chin, and area around the nostrils should be almost white. Nose leather is brick-red and paw pads are black. There is black hair between the toes, and black extends slightly beyond the paws on the hind feet.

Smoke Mau
The ground color of the Smoke Mau's coat is charcoal gray with a silver undercoat; markings are jet-black. Nose, lips, and eyes are outlined in black. The upper throat, chin, and the area around the nostrils should be the lightest charcoal gray color. Nose leather and paw pads are black. There is black hair between the toes, and black extends slightly beyond the paws on the hind feet.

Exotic Short-hair
The Exotic Short-hair was deliberately created by American breeders to fulfill a desire for a cat with the beauty of the Persian but without the problems associated with the Persian's long flowing coat.

The breed was produced through careful matings of American Short-hairs and Persians and is the only hybrid cross allowed today in the United States.

The Exotic Short-hair is identical to the Persian in conformation, with large round eyes, small ears, snub nose, cobby body, and short thick legs and tail.

The coat should be medium in length, dense, soft, and glossy. The Exotic Short-hair can occur in all the colors and patterns of Spectrum A.

German Rex
A cousin of the Cornish Rex, the German Rex was bred in Germany after the Second World War. During the 1950s it was used in developing the Rex breed in the United States.

Like the Cornish and Devon Rex, the coat is curly and without guard hairs.

Left: Egyptian Mau.

Havana Brown

The Havana Brown, an attractive, solid-color, mahogany-brown short-hair, was developed in England, where it is known as the Havana Foreign or Chestnut Brown Foreign. The name derives from the rich, warm color, which is close to that of Havana cigars.

These affectionate, soft-voiced cats make admirable pets. They often have the unusual habit of using their paws to investigate strange objects by touch, instead of relying on their sense of smell as do most other breeds. They are generally healthy animals, but do suffer in cold or damp weather.

The Havana's body is medium in length; firm and muscular with fine bones and graceful proportions. The legs are long and slim, with the hind legs slightly longer than the forelegs, and oval paws. The tail is also of medium length, with no sign of a kink.

The head is longer than it is wide with a distinct profile stop at the eyes, a fine rounded muzzle, and a definite break behind the whiskers. Ears are large and wide-set with slightly rounded tips; there is very little hair on either the outside or the inside. A Siamese head shape, a receding chin, and the lack of a profile stop at the eyes are all considered faults. Eyes are almond-shaped, slanting, and colored chartreuse green.

The coat is medium-length, smooth, and glossy; in color it is a rich, warm, chestnut or mahogany brown, as opposed to the shorter, darker, sable brown of the Burmese. The color must be even from nose to tail and from tip to root. White spots are considered faults. Whiskers should be brown; nose leather and paw pads are a rose color.

Left: Havana Brown.
Right: Cinnamon Oriental or Foreign, an unusual type of Oriental Short-hair.

Himalayan

The Himalayan is the fastest growing breed in the world today. It is a magnificent hybrid that combines Persian conformation and coat quality with Siamese colors and patterns.

The enormous amount of genetic research in the United States, Britain, and Scandinavia to produce the Himalayan was necessary in large part because both the desired characteristics — long hair and colorpoint pattern — are carried by recessive genes. In the United States breeders used Siamese and Persians, and although today Persian-Siamese crosses can be registered as Himalayans, in the near future only Persians will be permitted for use in Himalayan hybridization.

The Himalayan should have a Persian-type conformation: large round head with small ears, large round eyes, and deep nose break; cobby body; short, thick neck and legs; and large round paws. Any similarity to either the Siamese or the Peke-Face Persian is considered a fault. All Himalayans have deep blue eyes.

The coat should be long, thick, and soft, with a full frill. The four classic colors and patterns of Spectrum B (Blue Point, Chocolate Point, Lilac Point, and Seal Point) are recognized. In addition, Himalayans are recognized in Blue Cream Point, Flame Point, and Tortie Point.

Other colors of Himalayans are also being produced, but have not yet been admitted to the show bench. The three most popular are the Lynx Point, solid Chocolate, and solid Lilac.

Blue Cream Point Himalayan
The body color of this breed is bluish or creamy white, shading to white on chest and stomach; points are blue with patches of cream. Nose leather and paw pads are slate-blue, pink, or both.

Flame Point Himalayan
The body color of this breed is creamy white, with orange flame points. Nose leather and paw pads are flesh or coral pink.

Tortie Point Himalayan
The body color of this breed is creamy white or pale fawn; points are seal brown with un-brindled patches of red and cream. A red or cream blaze on the face is desirable. Nose leather and paw pads are seal brown with flesh or coral mottling.

Himbur
The Himbur is a hybrid produced in America by crossing the Himalayan with the Burmese. The Himbur is now recognized as a separate breed.

Japanese Bobtail
This is the indigenous cat of Japan, that originally came from China and Korea. It was imported into the US in 1969. A slender but muscular, medium-sized cat, the Japanese Bobtail has hind legs that are longer than its forelegs. They are angled, however, so that the body is nearly level when the cat is standing. The legs are long and slender but strong.

The Japanese Bobtail's distinctive tail is usually about 4 inches long and can be straight or curved. The hair on the tail is longer and thicker than the rest of the coat, and looks like a pom-pom.

The head is an equilateral triangle, with high cheek bones and a broad muzzle that curves into a distinct whisker break. Ears are large and wide-set at right angles to the head. Eyes are also large, oval, and slanted.

The coat is medium in length, soft, and silky. Preference is given to the traditional color: black and brilliant reddish-orange spots or shapes on a white ground. Colors of eyes, nose leather, and paw pads should harmonize with the coat as described in Spectrum A.

Above: Chocolate Point Himalayan.

44

Korat

The Korat, the good-luck cat of Thailand, came from the province of the same name.

The breed was exhibited in Britain as early as 1896 and a few were brought to the United States during the 1930s, but there were no serious attempts at breeding until the late 1950s. The Korat Cat Fanciers' Association was founded in 1965 to ensure that only those cats with Thai ancestry are registered.

Korats are rare even in Thailand; originally they could not be purchased, but had to be given as a gift. They are quiet, intelligent cats who take an active part in family life, but are apt to be nervous at shows.

The Korat is a hard, muscular, medium-sized cat. Its lines are all curves; it has a rounded back, well-proportioned legs (the hind legs are slightly longer than the front), and a medium-length tail that tapers to a rounded tip. A *non-visible* kink is permitted in show animals.

The head is heart-shaped, from the eyebrow ridges to the well-developed chin. There is a slight stop between the nose and the forehead, and the nose curves slightly downward just before the nose leather. Ears are very large, with rounded tips and a wide flare at the base. Eyes are also large; they are rounded when fully open but have an Oriental slant when partly or completely closed. Eyes should be a luminous green but an amber cast is acceptable.

The coat is close-lying and is silver blue in color tipped with silver. The tipping appears all over the coat especially where the hairs are shortest. The coat should be free of shading, tabby markings, and white spots. Nose leather and lips are dark blue or lavender. Paw pads range from dark blue to lavender with a pinkish tinge.

Maine Coon

Maine Coon Cats, according to New England experts, are the biggest, smartest, most beautiful cats in the world. According to legend, these thirty pound cats are part raccoon.

The body of a Maine Coon is large, muscular, broad-chested, and long, so that it has a rectangular shape. Legs should be medium in length, in good proportion to the body, and substantial. Paws are large, round and well-tufted; the tufts make it easy for the cat to 'snowshoe' across the frozen Maine countryside in winter. The tail is long and tapering.

The head is medium, with a square muzzle, high cheekbones, firm chin, and a medium-length nose. The ears, which are set high and well apart, are large, tapered, and tufted; 'Lynxline tips' (tufts on the tips of the ears) are especially desirable. Eyes are large and wide-set, slanting slightly upwards toward the ears.

Maine Coon Cats are penalized if they have a delicate bone structure, and are disqualified for having a receding chin, crossed eyes, a kinked tail, or an incorrect number of toes.

The coat is heavy and shaggy, shorter on the shoulders than on the stomach and haunches. The shagginess is most noticeable on the underparts and on the long-haired tail. There is a 'muttonchops' frill on the chest. Texture of the coat is silky and smooth. An even coat is a fault.

The Maine Coon Cat is bred and recognized in every color of Spectrum A (see Colors and Patterns); in addition, any color or combination of colors except those in Spectrum B is accepted. Eyes may be green, gold, or copper; in whites, eyes may also be blue or odd-eyed.

Manx

There are many myths about the tailless Manx: one, for example, tells how the Manx was very late for the Ark and had its tail cut off by an anxious Noah as he slammed the door shut.

In fact, the taillessness of this unique breed undoubtedly arose from a mutation within the small confines of the Isle of Man – a 221-square-mile island in the Irish Sea off the west coast of England.

The Manx makes a delightful pet – healthy, intelligent, and fond of people. It is also reputed to be an excellent ratter. Breeding Manx cats can be tricky, however. The mutation which causes the taillessness affects the vertebral column; if vertebrae are missing anywhere other than at the end, kittens will be born dead.

There are three variations found in Manx cats. *Rumpies* have no tail at all, and a hollow is found where the tail usually begins. Only Rumpies are accepted for show. *Stumpies* have one- to five-inch tails, and *Full-tails* or *Longies* have complete tails.

Over all, the Manx should give the impression of roundness. The body should be solid, compact, and well-balanced, with a round, broad chest, substantial round short front legs, and a round rump.

The hind legs are much longer than the forelegs, with a heavy, muscular thigh and a strong lower leg. In America Manx cats are disqualified for having a visible tail joint, polydactylism (wrong number of toes), or the inability to stand or walk properly.

The head is round, with prominent full cheeks and a rounded muzzle. Ears are wide-based, tapering, and rather long, but should be in proportion to the head.

The beautiful, plush coat is something like a rabbit's, with a short, thick, cottony undercoat and harder, glossier guard hairs.

The Manx is recognized in all the colors and patterns of Spectrum A (see Colors and Patterns), and in combination of colors and patterns which includes white. Eyes, nose leather, and paw pads should correspond with the coat color.

46

Manxamese

The Manxamese is a short-haired hybrid obtained by crossing Manx with Siamese to produce a cat with the colorpoint pattern of Spectrum B (see Colors and Patterns).

Ocicat

The Ocicat is a hybrid breed produced in America by mating a Siamese Chocolate Point male and an Abyssinian-Siamese crossbred female. It is now produced by crossing the Abyssinian with the American Short-hair, or either of these with the Ocicat itself. Although it is a recognized breed, it has not yet been accepted for championship competition.

The Ocicat has an Oriental conformation, with a head like the Abyssinian and golden oval eyes. The coat pattern is spots on a pale cream ground color, with tabby markings on the throat, legs, and tail. The markings are dark chestnut brown for the Dark Chestnut Ocicat or milk chocolate color for the Light Chestnut. The fur is short and silky.

Oriental Lavender

The Oriental Lavender is only produced when both parents carry genes for Blue and Chocolate. The coat should be frost-gray with a pinkish tone; eyes should be a rich green.

Oriental Short-hair

The Oriental Short-hair is a hybrid produced by crossing Siamese, American Short-hairs, Color-point Short-hairs, and other Oriental Short-hairs. It has the conformation of the Siamese (called 'Foreign' in Britain), but the colorpoint pattern has been eliminated. It has provisional acceptance from the American CFA.

Just as many breeders spent years trying to transfer the colorpoint pattern to Persian-type cats (see Himalayan), others are working to transfer the more exotic colors and patterns of Spectrum A (see Colors and Patterns) to the Siamese-type.

There are only a few minor differences between the Oriental Short-hair and Siamese standards. Males may be a bit larger than females; the tail is thin at the base; and cats are penalized for having crossed eyes. Oriental Short-hairs may have green or amber eyes in addition to bright blue.

Oriental Short-hairs are recognized in White, Ebony (Black), Blue, Chestnut (Self-Chocolate), Lavender (Lilac), Red, Cream, Silver, Cameo, Ebony (or Black) Smoke, Blue Smoke, Chestnut (or Chocolate) Smoke, Lavender Smoke, and Cameo (Red) Smoke and in Classic, Mackerel, and Spotted Tabby patterns.

Oriental White

Oriental Whites can be difficult, delicate cats, very prone to diseases.

The Oriental White should have a completely white coat with no trace of a colorpoint pattern. Eyes can be green or bright blue; gold-eyed cats are not accepted for the show bench. Paw pads and nose leather are pink.

Left: Oriental Short-hair kittens.
Inset: Oriental Lavender Queen and her kittens.

Above: Peke-faced Persian. Right: White Persian or Long-hair.

Peke-Face Persian

The Peke-Face Persian was developed in the United States during the 1930s from Standard Red and Red Tabby Persians. It is not recognized in England.

As the name suggests, the face should bear as close a resemblance as possible to that of the Pekinese dog, with a very short depressed nose, high forehead, large round eyes, and prominent ears. Peke-Face Persians often have deformed teeth and lower jaws, leading to difficulties in breathing. In all other respects, conformation should be that of the Persian.

Peke-Face Persians are only recognized in two colors: Red and Red Tabby.

Persian

The Persian is the aristocrat of domestic cats — the paragon of pedigreed breeds. The origin of the breed is obscure, but many experts believe that it first appeared in Persia and Turkey, and is a descendant of some Asian wild cat.

Persians are usually sedate and dignified cats. Their coats must be groomed daily to keep them free of loose hair, knots, tangles, and grease — and to keep the rugs and furniture relatively hairless. Show cats are usually groomed twice a day.

The Persian is a medium to large cat, but quality is more important than size. It has a cobby body: low-lying, long, and thick-set with a deep chest, massive shoulders and rump, and a short, well-rounded middle. The back is level and the legs short, thick, round and firm. Like all pedigree cats, the Persian has five toes on its front paws and four on its hind paws; polydactylism (an incorrect number of toes) is a fault. The tail is short and bushy, and should be in good proportion to the body. It is carried at an angle lower than the body, without curves.

The head, set on a short, thick neck, is round and massive, with full cheeks, powerful jaws, and a well-developed chin. The ears, which are small, wide-set, and tilted slightly forward, have long tufts of hair. The eyes are large, round, and set far apart. The nose is broad and short — almost snubby — and there should be a definite stop, or break, in the profile.

The Persian coat should be thick and soft, fine textured, with a glossy lively appearance. It should be long all over, including the shoulders; the ruff (longer hair around the head) should be immense, and continue down in a deep frill between the front legs. The condition and coloring of the coat is more important than body type. Persians are recognized in every color and pattern of Spectrum A (see Colors and Patterns), and Persian-type cats are also recognized in the colorpoint pattern of Spectrum B (see Himalayan).

Ragdolls

Ragdolls are a unique breed that derive their name from their limpness; when picked up they relax completely and flop over like a ragdoll. They are very placid creatures and completely fearless. This is, in fact, their weakness, for it puts them in great danger of injury, especially from other animals and children. They should never be allowed to wander or make contact with other animals, and require a great amount of care and attention.

Ragdolls are similar to Birmans, but are larger and have thicker fur. Markings are either Seal Point or Lilac Point with the Birmans' white boots and mittens.

Rex

The Rex is a spontaneous mutation of the domestic cat. Its short, tightly curled coat gives it an exotic appearance. Moreover, many people who are allergic to cat hairs find the Rex, because of its special coat, the perfect pet.

The Rex's arched back and muscular hind legs make it capable of attaining very high speeds as well as helping it make quick starts, changes of direction and high jumps. Its overall conformation is discussed in more detail in the entries for Cornish Rex and Devon Rex.

The coat, which is very important, is short, very soft and silky, and tightly curled due to the complete absence of guard hairs. This unique coat makes the Rex very warm to the touch.

Show cats are disqualified for having a kinked or abnormal tail, an incorrect number of toes, or any coarse guard hairs.

Most Rex colors are those described in Spectrum A (see Colors and Patterns), but Other Rex Colors (ORC) are also accepted for show.

Right: Solid Red.
Inset: Rex.

Russian Blue

Besides being beautiful, Russian Blues are quiet, shy, gentle animals that become firmly attached to their owners. They make lovely pets, especially in smaller houses or apartments.

The Russian Blue has fine bones and a long, lithe, sinuous body. Legs are long and the tail tapering. The neck is long and slender, though it appears short because of the thick fur on the neck and the animal's very high shoulder blades (ideally, the shoulder blades should almost touch behind the neck).

The head, which is short, should be wedge-shaped with a narrow, flat skull and a straight, receding forehead.

Scottish Fold

Mutations of cats with dropped ears have undoubtedly appeared at intervals throughout history, but the Scottish Fold, first discovered on a farm in Perthshire, Scotland in 1961, represents the first attempt to preserve the mutation.

It is a very appealing cat that is growing in popularity and has been recognized as a breed.

The Scottish Fold has a round, short, muscular body with a short, thick coat. The head is large with large round eyes and the ears have a distinctive fold.

Left: Russian Blue.
Inset left: Close-up of
Russian Blue.
Inset below: Scottish Fold.

Below: Lilac Point Siamese and her kitten.

Siamese

The Siamese, most popular of all the breeds, almost certainly originated in Siam (Thailand). Legend has it that they were bred by the Kings of Siam and used as palace guards.

In 1885 the first Siamese cat was exhibited at Crystal Palace in London. Siamese cats appeared in America around 1890 and were first exhibited in the early 1900s.

Much of the Siamese's popularity lies in its personality. They are intelligent, playful, individualistic animals, prone to demanding a lot of attention. They show much more open affection than other breeds and take easily to a lead. Most have a harsh voice; the queen's call when she is in heat can be loud and very disturbing.

Siamese have large litters (often as many as five kittens). Kittens are born white, with the points developing as the fur grows. Both females and males mature at a very early age, and care must be taken if females are to be kept from mating too early.

Siamese have been used in producing a surprising number of modern breeds including the Balinese, Bombay, Colorpoint Short-hair, Havana Brown, Himalayan, Lilac Foreign Short-hair, Manxamese, Oriental Short-hair, and Tonkinese.

The Siamese is a medium-sized cat with a long, slender, but muscular body and long slender legs. The body must be neither flabby nor bony; the tail is long, thin, and tapering; the paws oval and rather small.

The head should be a long, tapering wedge, medium-sized and in good proportion to the body. It narrows in straight lines to the muzzle and strong chin; there should be no whisker break. Allowances are made for jowls, however, in stud cats. The skull is flat; in profile there is a long straight line from the top of the head to the top of the nose.

The ears continue the lines of the wedge. They are very large, wide at the base, pointed, and pricked. Eyes are medium sized and almond-shaped, slanting toward the nose in lines that correspond with the shape of the wedge. Show cats cannot have crossed eyes, weak hind legs, mouth breathing due to nasal obstruction or a malformed jaw, emaciation, a visible tail kink, white toes and/or feet, and eyes that are any color but blue. Cats are penalized for having off-color or spotted paw pads or nose leather.

The coat is short, sleek, and close-lying. Siamese are recognized in the colorpoint pattern described in Colors and Patterns, but some notes of general interest about the various colors are appended below.

Blue Point Siamese

The Blue Point was the second variety of Siamese to gain recognition. There are early reports of its being seriously bred in England and America by the 1920s. The Blue Point is possibly more gentle than the other varieties, and loves to be hand-groomed. When grooming, take care not to brush too hard or too much; this will not only leave brush marks in the fur, but will also take out the undercoat.

Chocolate Point Siamese

The Chocolate Point is one of the earliest known varieties, but was only recognized in 1950. This was because the continual occurrence of blue in the points produced a much colder tone, leading people to believe that they were just Seal Points with poor coloration. The development of the colorpoints usually takes longer for Chocolate Point kittens than for other varieties, and the coat tends to grow far darker with age. Chocolate Point coats also react more to climatic conditions, making them difficult to breed and maintain in good condition.

Lilac (or Frost) Point Siamese

Lilac (or Frost) Points were first bred in America from parents who carried recessive genes for Blue and Chocolate. Coloration standards vary between Britain and America.

Seal Point Siamese

The Seal Point was the first Siamese variety to be recognized, and is still the most popular. The points begin to form on kittens as a smudge around the nose which becomes more definite as they grow; the line between mask and ears is not clearly defined until the cat is fully adult. The coat darkens with age on most cats and points are apt to develop brindling.

Smoke Persian

The Smoke Persian is probably the result of uncontrolled matings between White, Black, and Blue Persians around the turn of the century.

The dense, silky coat requires frequent grooming to remove loose hairs and keep it looking its best; the coat should be brushed away from the body.

Most Smoke Persians today are produced by mating Smoke to Smoke, though the type is sometimes improved by out-crossing to a Black. Kittens are born black.

Conformation should be that of the Persian; patterning is described in Colors and Patterns.

Blue Smoke Persians

These cats are recognized as a separate variety and result from mating Smoke and Blue Persians.

Right: Seal Point Siamese.
Inset: Smoke Persian.

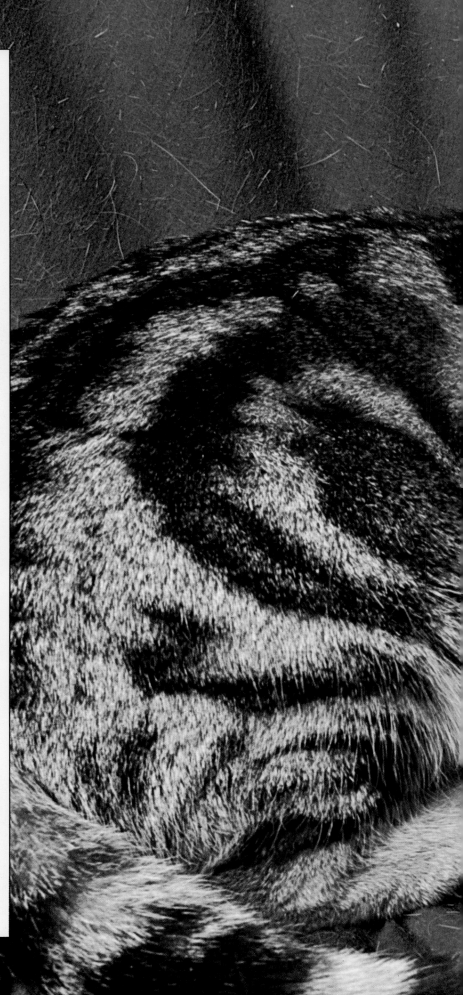

Smoke Short-hair

Black Smoke and Blue Smoke Short-hairs are recognized in the United States, but not in Britain; several European countries have provisional standards. The fur is short and white with black or blue tipping. Conformation should be that of the American Short-hair.

Solid Red

The Solid Red, also known as the Red Self or Red Persian, is rare because reproducing the coat color is very difficult; it is often more orange than deep red. Eliminating tabby markings, especially on the face, is also a major problem.

Somali

Somalis are long-haired Abyssinians that are rapidly becoming popular in America. They are slightly larger than short-haired Abyssinians and can be either red or ruddy. The coat is dense and requires comparatively little grooming; there should be a full ruff, with shorter hair on the shoulders. Somalis are quiet, affectionate cats with alert dispositions.

Sphynx

The Sphynx closely resembles the now-extinct Mexican Hairless.

This mutation was first recorded in 1966, born to a domestic Black and White in Ontario, Canada. The breed was developed from this specimen.

The Sphynx looks something like a sad, wrinkled Pug dog, and is very warm and smooth to the touch. Although they have been produced in the United States and Britain as well as in Canada, there does not appear to be much interest in the breed.

The body of the Sphynx is slender, with good muscles and a longish tail. The head is a rounded wedge shape with a short nose; ears are very wide at the base and slightly rounded at the tip; the eyes are golden and slightly slanted. The cat has no whiskers.

It may be any color, but solid colors must be even and parti-colors symmetrical. The face, ears, paws, and feet are covered with a fine short down, and there are hairs on the last inch of the tail.

Spotted Cat

Spotted Cats are a British short-haired breed. They are believed by some to have been the original domestic cat in that country. The breed died out, however, and it was not until 1960 that serious efforts (involving Silver Tabbies and Black Short-hairs) were made to recreate it.

The body of a show Spotted Cat should be of medium length, powerfully built, and thick set, with a full chest, and short, strong legs. The tail is rather short, and thick at the base, tapering slightly at the tip.

The head should be broad with well-developed cheeks, small slightly rounded ears, and large round eyes that compliment the coat color.

The coat is short and fine. The markings must be distinct spots that contrast well with the ground color; they may be round or oblong, but bars or even broken stripes are considered faults. The spots should cover the entire body. Tabby markings on the face and head are acceptable.

Spotted Cats can be any color in Spectrum A (see Colors and Patterns) as long as there is good contrast between ground color and markings. Brown, Red, and Silver are the most popular colors.

Supilak
The Supilak, or Copper, is a copper-colored cat from Thailand. It has been recognized as a breed in America, but is not eligible for show competition.

Tabby
The term 'Tabby' is usually applied to any cat with stripes and bars, although the standard for show cats is quite specific about the desired patterning (see Colors and Patterns). It has been claimed that if all the domestic cats in the world were to interbreed, eventually all cats would be tabbies. The 'M' on the forehead is said to be the mark of Mohammed.

The standard for markings applies to both Tabby Persians and Tabby Short-hairs. The two patterns, Classic and Mackerel, are classed together in Britain and separately in the United States. Conformation should be that of either the Persian or the appropriate short-hair. The most common Tabby varieties are Brown, Red, and Silver; in America, Tabbies are also recognized in Blue, Cameo and Cream.

Brown Tabby Persian
Once very popular, Brown Tabby Persians have become difficult to breed and today few are shown. If like-to-like mating is impossible, the best results will be achieved by mating a Brown Tabby with a Black or a dark Blue and then back to a Brown Tabby. Silver Tabbies lighten the ground color and discolor the eyes; Red Tabbies tend to weaken the conformation. Brindling is becoming a common fault in Brown Tabby Persians.

Red Tabby Persian
Some people believe that this is a male only cat; however, Red to Red mating will produce both sexes.

Left: An adult Brown Tabby Short-hair on show.

Silver Tabby Persian

This breed is no longer popular since it is extremely difficult to perfect. Often the markings are smudged and unclear, and brown or bronze tinges tend to creep into the coloring. There is also a problem in finding a mate that will improve the conformation without damaging the markings. Kittens are born nearly all black, and the silver appears after about four months. Kittens *born* with tabby markings often prove to be badly patterned adults.

Blue Tabby Persian

This breed was officially recognized in America in 1962 and first appeared in Brown Tabby litters.

Brown Tabby Short-hair

One of the oldest known breeds, this cat's appearance as a pedigreed cat is relatively rare. It is rather difficult to find the right stud; like-to-like matings are likely to lead to deterioration of conformation.

Red Tabby Short-hair

These cats are often marmalade, ginger, or sandy cats. Red Tabby males are often mated with Tortoiseshells or Calicos (both virtually all-female varieties), though it sometimes is difficult to eliminate the tabby markings once they have been introduced.

Silver Tabby Short-hair

The Silver Tabby Short-hair is the most popular of the Tabby Short-hairs. Kittens are born with clear markings that fade and then re-establish themselves at about three months. Silver Tabby conformation is usually better than that of the other types, and Blacks are often introduced to maintain the standard.

Tonkinese

The Tonkinese was produced in the United States by crossing a Siamese and a Burmese. It is now being bred on both sides of the Atlantic, in Australia and New Zealand, but has not been recognized.

Tortoiseshell Persian

The coat of this striking cat should be long and patterned with distinct patches of deep rich black, red, and cream. Black should not be predominant.

Tri-colored cats are one of the oldest known varieties, but they were usually products of random matings. However, cats with tabby markings, stray white hairs, and blurred, indistinct patches, are usually unacceptable as show cats.

The Tortoiseshell Persian is very difficult to reproduce to the high standard required of show cats. It is virtually an all female breed (the few males born are always sterile), so like-to-like breeding is impossible. Instead, breeders must use a Black or Cream male and a Tortie female, with completely unpredictable results.

Conformation should be that of the Persian.

Tortoiseshell Short-hair

Tortoiseshell Short-hairs should conform to the short-hair standard (see American Short-hair or British Short-hair), with the markings described in Colors and Patterns. Breeding these attractive, playful cats is subject to the same uncertainties described for the Tortoiseshell Persian.

Left: Tortoiseshell and White Short-hair (Calico).
Inset: Tortoiseshell Persian.

Turkish Van Cat

The Turkish Van Cat comes from the Lake Van area of Turkey where it has been kept as a domestic pet for centuries. It is also known as the Van Cat or Swimming Cat. This cat loves nothing more than a swim or a bath in warm water, although care must be taken to see that the animal is thoroughly dried after its dip to prevent colds.

Litters usually consist of only two kittens which are, more often than not, males. Kittens are born with markings that are usually more pronounced than in adults.

The conformation of the Turkish Van Cat is similar to the Angora. It should have a long, sturdy body on medium-length legs; a thick, muscular neck and shoulders; a blunt, medium-length tail; round paws with tufted toes; and a small wedge-shaped head. The ears are large and rounded and are set upright, quite close together. The eyes are round and the nose rather long.

The coat consists of a wooly undercoat and long, silky hairs. The color should be chalk white without any yellowish traces. There are auburn splotches on the head and auburn rings on the tail. The background color on the tail is a lighter shade of auburn. Ears are white with a slight pinkish tinge on the inside. Nose leather and paw pads are shell pink.

White Persian

This beautiful and popular variety owes much of its development to the Angora. Thus, its conformation differs a bit from the Persian standards: its body is slightly longer, the face not quite so round, the ears slightly larger and the nose longer.

The long, silky coat should be pure white; any yellow staining is a fault.

Whites are usually bred by mating Whites with Blacks, Blues, or Creams. Like-to-like mating is difficult and must be carefully planned.

Although they are a fastidious variety, they do require frequent grooming. A warm bath a few days before a show will vastly improve their appearance. There are three recognized types of White Persian, based solely on eye color.

Blue-Eyed White

This type of White Persian was the first to be bred. Unfortunately they are almost always deaf. Until recently, this type was rapidly declining in numbers, but breeders are now making a determined effort to re-establish it by introducing Blue Persians and the other two White varieties into their breeding programs. Cats born with a small dark smudge on the underparts usually have good hearing, and there is also the possibility that the smudge will fade as they mature making them suitable for showing. The blue eye color is difficult to reproduce; green eyes are a fault.

Odd-Eyed White

This breed appears in litters of both Blue-Eyed and Orange-Eyed Whites. They were recognized in Britain in 1968. They are not deaf, though many claim that they are hard of hearing on the side that has the blue eye. Conformation is generally better than in Blue-Eyed Whites.

Orange-Eyed White

This breed resulted from a chance mating between a Blue-Eyed White and another Persian with orange eyes. They were recognized during the 1930s. Their breeding is much more predictable than for the Blue-Eyed; they usually have a better conformation; they are not deaf.

White Short-hair

Conformation should be that of the short-hair standard. The coat should be fine and soft, pure white with no trace of colored hairs and no tinge of yellow. Like the White Persian, the White Short-hair is recognized in three varieties based on eye color.

Blue-Eyed White

This popular, but rather rare cat is hard to breed with outstanding conformation. Most Blue-Eyed Whites are deaf; those with a dark smudge on their heads between the ears usually have good hearing.

Odd-Eyed White

This breed with one blue eye and one orange, is not deaf, and plays a useful role in breeding both other varieties. They can be found in both Blue-Eyed and Orange-Eyed litters.

Orange-Eyed White

Like the other White Short-hairs, Orange-Eyed Whites are born with blue eyes which then, however, turn slowly to orange as the cat matures. The orange deepens with age and often turns to a coppery color in adulthood. This variety has good hearing.

Left: Turkish Van Cat.
Below: A young White Short-hair.
Overleaf: White Blue-eyed Persian kitten.

64